New Product Workbook

Name: _____

Date: _____

Product	Date
1	
2	
3	
4	
5	
6	
7	
8	
9	
10	
11	
12	
13	
14	
15	
16	
17	
18	
19	
20	

Product	Date
21	
22	
23	
24	
25	
26	
27	
28	
29	
30	
31	
32	
33	
34	
35	
36	
37	
38	
39	
40	

New Product Worksheets

Product Name #

Overview

Outline of product

Specifics (weight, size)

Materials

Other (ie color, fragrance)

Standalone Product ☐   Product Range ☐

Features   ### Benefits

-
-
-
-
-

Ideal Customer / Target Market

Need / Want / Problem this product is addressing

Competitor Products

Points of Difference

Materials & Suppliers

Material	Supplier	Cost
●	●	●
●	●	●
●	●	●
●	●	●
●	●	●

Pricing

$ $ $

Materials Cost   Sale Price   Margin

Overheads

Other   (Sale Price - Base Cost)

Labor

Base Cost   _____

Shipping and packaging

Note: If offering 'free shipping' remember to add this to your base cost

Marketing

Keywords

Marketing Plan Outline

Social Media Post & Graphics Ideas

Newsletter Headline & Content ideas

Promotion Ideas

Notes

Product Name

Overview

Outline of product

Specifics (weight, size)

Materials

Other (ie color, fragrance)

Standalone Product ☐   Product Range ☐

Features   Benefits
-
-
-
-
-

Ideal Customer / Target Market

Need / Want / Problem this product is addressing

Competitor Products

Points of Difference

Materials & Suppliers

Material   Supplier   Cost
-
-
-
-
-

Pricing

$ $ $

Materials Cost   Sale Price   Margin

Overheads

Other   (Sale Price - Base Cost)

Labor

Base Cost   _____

Shipping and packaging

Note: If offering 'free shipping' remember to add this to your base cost

Marketing

Keywords

Marketing Plan Outline

Social Media Post & Graphics Ideas

Newsletter Headline & Content ideas

Promotion Ideas

Notes

Product Name

Overview

Outline of product

Specifics (weight, size)

Materials

Other (ie color, fragrance)

Standalone Product ☐   Product Range ☐

Features

-
-
-
-
-

Benefits

-
-
-
-
-

Ideal Customer / Target Market

Need / Want / Problem this product is addressing

Competitor Products

Points of Difference

Materials & Suppliers

Material	Supplier	Cost

Pricing

$ $ $

Materials Cost   Sale Price   Margin

Overheads

Other   (Sale Price - Base Cost)

Labor

Base Cost   _____

Shipping and packaging

Note: If offering 'free shipping' remember to add this to your base cost

Marketing

Keywords

Marketing Plan Outline

Social Media Post & Graphics Ideas

Newsletter Headline & Content ideas

Promotion Ideas

Notes

Product Name

Overview

Outline of product

Specifics (weight, size)

Materials

Other (ie color, fragrance)

Standalone Product ☐   Product Range ☐

Features	Benefits
●	●
●	●
●	●
●	●
●	●

Ideal Customer / Target Market

Need / Want / Problem this product is addressing

Competitor Products

Points of Difference

Materials & Suppliers

Material	Supplier	Cost
●	●	●
●	●	●
●	●	●
●	●	●
●	●	●

Pricing

$ $ $

Materials Cost   Sale Price   Margin

Overheads

Other   (Sale Price - Base Cost)

Labor

_____

Base Cost   _____

Shipping and packaging

Note: If offering 'free shipping' remember to add this to your base cost

Marketing

Keywords

Marketing Plan Outline

Social Media Post & Graphics Ideas

Newsletter Headline & Content ideas

Promotion Ideas

Notes

Product Name

Overview

Outline of product

Specifics (weight, size)

Materials

Other (ie color, fragrance)

Standalone Product ☐   Product Range ☐

Features	Benefits
•	•
•	•
•	•
•	•
•	•

Ideal Customer / Target Market

Need / Want / Problem this product is addressing

Competitor Products

Points of Difference

Materials & Suppliers

Material	Supplier	Cost
•	•	•
•	•	•
•	•	•
•	•	•
•	•	•

Pricing

$

Materials Cost
Overheads
Other
Labor

$

Sale Price

$

Margin

(Sale Price - Base Cost)

Base Cost   _____

Shipping and packaging
Note: If offering 'free shipping' remember to add this to your base cost

Marketing

Keywords

Marketing Plan Outline

Social Media Post & Graphics Ideas

Newsletter Headline & Content ideas

Promotion Ideas

Notes

Product Name

Overview

Outline of product

Specifics (weight, size)

Materials

Other (ie color, fragrance)

Standalone Product ☐   Product Range ☐

Features	Benefits
•	•
•	•
•	•
•	•
•	•

Ideal Customer / Target Market

Need / Want / Problem this product is addressing

Competitor Products

Points of Difference

Materials & Suppliers

Material	Supplier	Cost
•	•	•
•	•	•
•	•	•
•	•	•
•	•	•

Pricing

$ $ $

Materials Cost   Sale Price   Margin
Overheads
Other   (Sale Price - Base Cost)
Labor

Base Cost   _____

Shipping and packaging
Note: If offering 'free shipping' remember to add this to your base cost

Marketing

Keywords

Marketing Plan Outline

Social Media Post & Graphics Ideas

Newsletter Headline & Content ideas

Promotion Ideas

Notes

Product Name

Overview

Outline of product

Specifics (weight, size)

Materials

Other (ie color, fragrance)

Standalone Product ☐   Product Range ☐

Features

-
-
-
-
-

Benefits

-
-
-
-
-

Ideal Customer / Target Market

Need / Want / Problem this product is addressing

Competitor Products

Points of Difference

Materials & Suppliers

Material	Supplier	Cost
•	•	•
•	•	•
•	•	•
•	•	•
•	•	•

Pricing

	$		$		$
Materials Cost		Sale Price		Margin	
Overheads					
Other				(Sale Price - Base Cost)	
Labor					

Base Cost _____

Shipping and packaging
Note: If offering 'free shipping' remember to add this to your base cost

Marketing

Keywords

Marketing Plan Outline

Social Media Post & Graphics Ideas

Newsletter Headline & Content ideas

Promotion Ideas

Notes

Product Name

Overview

Outline of product

Specifics (weight, size)

Materials

Other (ie color, fragrance)

Standalone Product ☐   Product Range ☐

Features
-
-
-
-
-

Benefits
-
-
-
-

Ideal Customer / Target Market

Need / Want / Problem this product is addressing

Competitor Products

Points of Difference

Materials & Suppliers

Material	Supplier	Cost

Pricing

$ $ $

Materials Cost   Sale Price   Margin

Overheads

Other   (Sale Price - Base Cost)

Labor

Base Cost   _____

Shipping and packaging

Note: If offering 'free shipping' remember to add this to your base cost

Marketing

Keywords

Marketing Plan Outline

Social Media Post & Graphics Ideas

Newsletter Headline & Content ideas

Promotion Ideas

Notes

Product Name

Overview

Outline of product

Specifics (weight, size)

Materials

Other (ie color, fragrance)

Standalone Product ☐   Product Range ☐

Features	Benefits
•	•
•	•
•	•
•	•
•	•

Ideal Customer / Target Market

Need / Want / Problem this product is addressing

Competitor Products

Points of Difference

Materials & Suppliers

Material	Supplier	Cost
•	•	•
•	•	•
•	•	•
•	•	•
•	•	•

Pricing

$ $ $

Materials Cost   Sale Price   Margin

Overheads

Other   (Sale Price - Base Cost)

Labor

Base Cost   _____

Shipping and packaging

Note: If offering 'free shipping' remember to add this to your base cost

Marketing

Keywords

Marketing Plan Outline

Social Media Post & Graphics Ideas

Newsletter Headline & Content ideas

Promotion Ideas

Notes

Product Name

Overview

Outline of product

Specifics (weight, size)

Materials

Other (ie color, fragrance)

Standalone Product ☐   Product Range ☐

Features	Benefits
•	•
•	•
•	•
•	•
•	•

Ideal Customer / Target Market

Need / Want / Problem this product is addressing

Competitor Products

Points of Difference

Materials & Suppliers

Material	Supplier	Cost
•	•	•
•	•	•
•	•	•
•	•	•
•	•	•

Pricing

$ $ $

Materials Cost   Sale Price   Margin

Overheads

Other   (Sale Price - Base Cost)

Labor

_____

Base Cost   _____

Shipping and packaging

Note: If offering 'free shipping' remember to add this to your base cost

Marketing

Keywords

Marketing Plan Outline

Social Media Post & Graphics Ideas

Newsletter Headline & Content ideas

Promotion Ideas

Notes

Product Name

Overview

Outline of product

Specifics (weight, size)

Materials

Other (ie color, fragrance)

Standalone Product ☐   Product Range ☐

Features

-
-
-
-
-

Benefits

-
-
-
-
-

Ideal Customer / Target Market

Need / Want / Problem this product is addressing

Competitor Products

Points of Difference

Materials & Suppliers

Material	Supplier	Cost

Pricing

$ $ $

Materials Cost   Sale Price   Margin

Overheads

Other   (Sale Price - Base Cost)

Labor

Base Cost   _____

Shipping and packaging

Note: If offering 'free shipping' remember to add this to your base cost

Marketing

Keywords

Marketing Plan Outline

Social Media Post & Graphics Ideas

Newsletter Headline & Content ideas

Promotion Ideas

Notes

Product Name

Overview

Outline of product

Specifics (weight, size)

Materials

Other (ie color, fragrance)

Standalone Product ☐   Product Range ☐

Features   ### Benefits

-
-
-
-
-

Ideal Customer / Target Market

Need / Want / Problem this product is addressing

Competitor Products

Points of Difference

Materials & Suppliers

Material	Supplier	Cost

Pricing

$ $ $

Materials Cost   Sale Price   Margin
Overheads
Other   (Sale Price - Base Cost)
Labor

Base Cost   _____

Shipping and packaging
Note: If offering 'free shipping' remember to add this to your base cost

Marketing

Keywords

Marketing Plan Outline

Social Media Post & Graphics Ideas

Newsletter Headline & Content ideas

Promotion Ideas

Notes

Product Name

Overview

Outline of product

Specifics (weight, size)

Materials

Other (ie color, fragrance)

Standalone Product ☐   Product Range ☐

Features   ### Benefits

-
-
-
-
-

-
-
-
-
-

Ideal Customer / Target Market

Need / Want / Problem this product is addressing

Competitor Products

Points of Difference

Materials & Suppliers

Material	Supplier	Cost
•	•	•
•	•	•
•	•	•
•	•	•
•	•	•

Pricing

$ $ $

Materials Cost   Sale Price   Margin

Overheads

Other   (Sale Price - Base Cost)

Labor

Base Cost _____

Shipping and packaging

Note: If offering 'free shipping' remember to add this to your base cost

Marketing

Keywords

Marketing Plan Outline

Social Media Post & Graphics Ideas

Newsletter Headline & Content ideas

Promotion Ideas

Notes

Product Name

Overview

Outline of product

Specifics (weight, size)

Materials

Other (ie color, fragrance)

Standalone Product ☐   Product Range ☐

Features	Benefits
●	●
●	●
●	●
●	●
●	●

Ideal Customer / Target Market

Need / Want / Problem this product is addressing

Competitor Products

Points of Difference

Materials & Suppliers

Material	Supplier	Cost
●	●	●
●	●	●
●	●	●
●	●	●
●	●	●

Pricing

$	$	$
Materials Cost	Sale Price	Margin
Overheads		
Other		(Sale Price - Base Cost)
Labor		

Base Cost _____

Shipping and packaging
Note: If offering 'free shipping' remember to add this to your base cost

Marketing

Keywords

Marketing Plan Outline

Social Media Post & Graphics Ideas

Newsletter Headline & Content ideas

Promotion Ideas

Notes

Product Name

Overview

Outline of product

Specifics (weight, size)

Materials

Other (ie color, fragrance)

Standalone Product ☐   Product Range ☐

Features   Benefits
-
-
-
-
-

-
-
-
-
-

Ideal Customer / Target Market

Need / Want / Problem this product is addressing

Competitor Products

Points of Difference

Materials & Suppliers

Material	Supplier	Cost
•	•	•
•	•	•
•	•	•
•	•	•
•	•	•

Pricing

$ $ $

Materials Cost   Sale Price   Margin

Overheads

Other   (Sale Price - Base Cost)

Labor

Base Cost   _____

Shipping and packaging

Note: If offering 'free shipping' remember to add this to your base cost

Marketing

Keywords

Marketing Plan Outline

Social Media Post & Graphics Ideas

Newsletter Headline & Content ideas

Promotion Ideas

Notes

Product Name

Overview

Outline of product

Specifics (weight, size)

Materials

Other (ie color, fragrance)

Standalone Product ☐   Product Range ☐

Features	Benefits
•	•
•	•
•	•
•	•
•	•

Ideal Customer / Target Market

Need / Want / Problem this product is addressing

Competitor Products

Points of Difference

Materials & Suppliers

Material	Supplier	Cost
•	•	•
•	•	•
•	•	•
•	•	•
•	•	•

Pricing

$ $ $

Materials Cost   Sale Price   Margin

Overheads

Other   (Sale Price - Base Cost)

Labor

Base Cost   _____

Shipping and packaging

Note: If offering 'free shipping' remember to add this to your base cost

Marketing

Keywords

Marketing Plan Outline

Social Media Post & Graphics Ideas

Newsletter Headline & Content ideas

Promotion Ideas

Notes

Product Name

Overview

Outline of product

Specifics (weight, size)

Materials

Other (ie color, fragrance)

Standalone Product ☐   Product Range ☐

Features

-
-
-
-
-

Benefits

-
-
-
-
-

Ideal Customer / Target Market

Need / Want / Problem this product is addressing

Competitor Products

Points of Difference

Materials & Suppliers

Material	Supplier	Cost
•	•	•
•	•	•
•	•	•
•	•	•
•	•	•

Pricing

$ $ $

Materials Cost   Sale Price   Margin

Overheads

Other   (Sale Price - Base Cost)

Labor

Base Cost   _____

Shipping and packaging

Note: If offering 'free shipping' remember to add this to your base cost

Marketing

Keywords

Marketing Plan Outline

Social Media Post & Graphics Ideas

Newsletter Headline & Content ideas

Promotion Ideas

Notes

Product Name

Overview

Outline of product

Specifics (weight, size)

Materials

Other (ie color, fragrance)

Standalone Product ☐   Product Range ☐

Features
-
-
-
-
-

Benefits
-
-
-
-
-

Ideal Customer / Target Market

Need / Want / Problem this product is addressing

Competitor Products

Points of Difference

Materials & Suppliers

Material	Supplier	Cost
•	•	•
•	•	•
•	•	•
•	•	•
•	•	•

Pricing

$ $ $

Materials Cost   Sale Price   Margin

Overheads

Other   (Sale Price - Base Cost)

Labor

Base Cost   _____

Shipping and packaging

Note: If offering 'free shipping' remember to add this to your base cost

Marketing

Keywords

Marketing Plan Outline

Social Media Post & Graphics Ideas

Newsletter Headline & Content ideas

Promotion Ideas

Notes

Product Name

Overview

Outline of product

Specifics (weight, size)

Materials

Other (ie color, fragrance)

Standalone Product ☐   Product Range ☐

Features   ### Benefits

-
-
-
-
-

Ideal Customer / Target Market

Need / Want / Problem this product is addressing

Competitor Products

Points of Difference

Materials & Suppliers

Material   ### Supplier   ### Cost

-
-
-
-
-

Pricing

$ $ $

Materials Cost   Sale Price   Margin

Overheads

Other   (Sale Price - Base Cost)

Labor

Base Cost   _____

Shipping and packaging

Note: If offering 'free shipping' remember to add this to your base cost

Marketing

Keywords

Marketing Plan Outline

Social Media Post & Graphics Ideas

Newsletter Headline & Content ideas

Promotion Ideas

Notes

Product Name

Overview

Outline of product

Specifics (weight, size)

Materials

Other (ie color, fragrance)

Standalone Product ☐   Product Range ☐

Features

-
-
-
-
-

Benefits

-
-
-
-
-

Ideal Customer / Target Market

Need / Want / Problem this product is addressing

Competitor Products

Points of Difference

Materials & Suppliers

Material	Supplier	Cost
•	•	•
•	•	•
•	•	•
•	•	•
•	•	•

Pricing

$ $ $

Materials Cost   Sale Price   Margin
Overheads
Other   (Sale Price - Base Cost)
Labor

Base Cost   _____

Shipping and packaging
Note: If offering 'free shipping' remember to add this to your base cost

Marketing

Keywords

Marketing Plan Outline

Social Media Post & Graphics Ideas

Newsletter Headline & Content ideas

Promotion Ideas

Notes

Product Name #

Overview

Outline of product

Specifics (weight, size)

Materials

Other (ie color, fragrance)

Standalone Product ☐   Product Range ☐

Features

-
-
-
-
-

Benefits

-
-
-
-
-

Ideal Customer / Target Market

Need / Want / Problem this product is addressing

Competitor Products

Points of Difference

Materials & Suppliers

Material	Supplier	Cost
•	•	•
•	•	•
•	•	•
•	•	•
•	•	•

Pricing

	$		$		$
Materials Cost		Sale Price		Margin	
Overheads					
Other				(Sale Price - Base Cost)	
Labor					

Base Cost _____

Shipping and packaging

Note: If offering 'free shipping' remember to add this to your base cost

Marketing

Keywords

Marketing Plan Outline

Social Media Post & Graphics Ideas

Newsletter Headline & Content ideas

Promotion Ideas

Notes

Product Name

Overview

Outline of product

Specifics (weight, size)

Materials

Other (ie color, fragrance)

Standalone Product ☐   Product Range ☐

Features	Benefits
•	•
•	•
•	•
•	•
•	•

Ideal Customer / Target Market

Need / Want / Problem this product is addressing

Competitor Products

Points of Difference

Materials & Suppliers

Material	Supplier	Cost
•	•	•
•	•	•
•	•	•
•	•	•
•	•	•

Pricing

$

Materials Cost
Overheads
Other
Labor

Base Cost _____

Shipping and packaging
Note: If offering 'free shipping' remember to add this to your base cost

$

Sale Price

$

Margin

(Sale Price - Base Cost)

Marketing

Keywords

Marketing Plan Outline

Social Media Post & Graphics Ideas

Newsletter Headline & Content ideas

Promotion Ideas

Notes

Product Name

Overview

Outline of product

Specifics (weight, size)

Materials

Other (ie color, fragrance)

Standalone Product ☐   Product Range ☐

Features	Benefits
•	•
•	•
•	•
•	•
•	•

Ideal Customer / Target Market

Need / Want / Problem this product is addressing

Competitor Products

Points of Difference

Materials & Suppliers

Material	Supplier	Cost
•	•	•
•	•	•
•	•	•
•	•	•
•	•	•

Pricing

$ $ $

Materials Cost   Sale Price   Margin

Overheads

Other   (Sale Price - Base Cost)

Labor

Base Cost   _____

Shipping and packaging

Note: If offering 'free shipping' remember to add this to your base cost

Marketing

Keywords

Marketing Plan Outline

Social Media Post & Graphics Ideas

Newsletter Headline & Content ideas

Promotion Ideas

Notes

Product Name

Overview

Outline of product

Specifics (weight, size)

Materials

Other (ie color, fragrance)

Standalone Product ☐   Product Range ☐

Features	Benefits
•	•
•	•
•	•
•	•
•	•

Ideal Customer / Target Market

Need / Want / Problem this product is addressing

Competitor Products

Points of Difference

Materials & Suppliers

Material	Supplier	Cost
•	•	•
•	•	•
•	•	•
•	•	•
•	•	•

Pricing

$ $ $

Materials Cost   Sale Price   Margin

Overheads

Other   (Sale Price - Base Cost)

Labor

Base Cost   ————————

Shipping and packaging

Note: If offering 'free shipping' remember to add this to your base cost

Marketing

Keywords

Marketing Plan Outline

Social Media Post & Graphics Ideas

Newsletter Headline & Content ideas

Promotion Ideas

Notes

Product Name

Overview

Outline of product

Specifics (weight, size)

Materials

Other (ie color, fragrance)

Standalone Product ☐   Product Range ☐

Features	Benefits
•	•
•	•
•	•
•	•
•	•

Ideal Customer / Target Market

Need / Want / Problem this product is addressing

Competitor Products

Points of Difference

Materials & Suppliers

Material	Supplier	Cost
•	•	•
•	•	•
•	•	•
•	•	•
•	•	•

Pricing

$

Materials Cost
Overheads
Other
Labor

Sale Price $

Margin $

(Sale Price - Base Cost)

Base Cost _____

_____

Shipping and packaging
Note: If offering 'free shipping' remember to add this to your base cost

Marketing

Keywords

Marketing Plan Outline

Social Media Post & Graphics Ideas

Newsletter Headline & Content ideas

Promotion Ideas

Notes

Product Name

Overview

Outline of product

Specifics (weight, size)

Materials

Other (ie color, fragrance)

Standalone Product ☐   Product Range ☐

Features

-
-
-
-
-

Benefits

-
-
-
-
-

Ideal Customer / Target Market

Need / Want / Problem this product is addressing

Competitor Products

Points of Difference

Materials & Suppliers

Material	Supplier	Cost

Pricing

$ $ $

Materials Cost   Sale Price   Margin

Overheads

Other   (Sale Price - Base Cost)

Labor

_____

Base Cost   _____

Shipping and packaging

Note: If offering 'free shipping' remember to add this to your base cost

Marketing

Keywords

Marketing Plan Outline

Social Media Post & Graphics Ideas

Newsletter Headline & Content ideas

Promotion Ideas

Notes

Product Name

Overview

Outline of product

Specifics (weight, size)

Materials

Other (ie color, fragrance)

Standalone Product ☐   Product Range ☐

Features   ### Benefits

-
-
-
-
-

-
-
-
-
-

Ideal Customer / Target Market

Need / Want / Problem this product is addressing

Competitor Products

Points of Difference

Materials & Suppliers

Material	Supplier	Cost
•	•	•
•	•	•
•	•	•
•	•	•
•	•	•

Pricing

$ $ $

Materials Cost   Sale Price   Margin

Overheads

Other   (Sale Price - Base Cost)

Labor

Base Cost   _____

Shipping and packaging

Note: If offering 'free shipping' remember to add this to your base cost

Marketing

Keywords

Marketing Plan Outline

Social Media Post & Graphics Ideas

Newsletter Headline & Content ideas

Promotion Ideas

Notes

Product Name

Overview

Outline of product

Specifics (weight, size)

Materials

Other (ie color, fragrance)

Standalone Product ☐   Product Range ☐

Features	Benefits
•	•
•	•
•	•
•	•
•	•

Ideal Customer / Target Market

Need / Want / Problem this product is addressing

Competitor Products

Points of Difference

Materials & Suppliers

Material	Supplier	Cost
•	•	•
•	•	•
•	•	•
•	•	•
•	•	•

Pricing

$ $ $

Materials Cost   Sale Price   Margin

Overheads

Other   (Sale Price - Base Cost)

Labor

Base Cost _____

Shipping and packaging

Note: If offering 'free shipping' remember to add this to your base cost

Marketing

Keywords

Marketing Plan Outline

Social Media Post & Graphics Ideas

Newsletter Headline & Content ideas

Promotion Ideas

Notes

Product Name

Overview

Outline of product

Specifics (weight, size)

Materials

Other (ie color, fragrance)

Standalone Product ☐   Product Range ☐

Features	Benefits
•	•
•	•
•	•
•	•
•	•

Ideal Customer / Target Market

Need / Want / Problem this product is addressing

Competitor Products

Points of Difference

Materials & Suppliers

Material	Supplier	Cost
•	•	•
•	•	•
•	•	•
•	•	•
•	•	•

Pricing

$ $ $

Materials Cost   Sale Price   Margin

Overheads

Other   (Sale Price - Base Cost)

Labor

Base Cost _____

Shipping and packaging

Note: If offering 'free shipping' remember to add this to your base cost

Marketing

Keywords

Marketing Plan Outline

Social Media Post & Graphics Ideas

Newsletter Headline & Content ideas

Promotion Ideas

Notes

Product Name

Overview

Outline of product

Specifics (weight, size)

Materials

Other (ie color, fragrance)

Standalone Product ☐   Product Range ☐

Features   Benefits

-
-
-
-
-

Ideal Customer / Target Market

Need / Want / Problem this product is addressing

Competitor Products

Points of Difference

Materials & Suppliers

Material	Supplier	Cost
•	•	•
•	•	•
•	•	•
•	•	•
•	•	•

Pricing

$ $ $

Materials Cost   Sale Price   Margin
Overheads
Other   (Sale Price - Base Cost)
Labor

Base Cost   _____

Shipping and packaging
Note: If offering 'free shipping' remember to add this to your base cost

Marketing

Keywords

Marketing Plan Outline

Social Media Post & Graphics Ideas

Newsletter Headline & Content ideas

Promotion Ideas

Notes

Product Name

Overview

Outline of product

Specifics (weight, size)

Materials

Other (ie color, fragrance)

Standalone Product ☐   Product Range ☐

Features	Benefits
•	•
•	•
•	•
•	•
•	•

Ideal Customer / Target Market

Need / Want / Problem this product is addressing

Competitor Products

Points of Difference

Materials & Suppliers

Material	Supplier	Cost
•	•	•
•	•	•
•	•	•
•	•	•
•	•	•

Pricing

$

Materials Cost
Overheads
Other
Labor

$ Sale Price

$ Margin

(Sale Price - Base Cost)

Base Cost _____

Shipping and packaging
Note: If offering 'free shipping' remember to add this to your base cost

Marketing

Keywords

Marketing Plan Outline

Social Media Post & Graphics Ideas

Newsletter Headline & Content ideas

Promotion Ideas

Notes

Product Name

Overview

Outline of product

Specifics (weight, size)

Materials

Other (ie color, fragrance)

Standalone Product ☐   Product Range ☐

Features   ### Benefits

-
-
-
-
-

-
-
-
-
-

Ideal Customer / Target Market

Need / Want / Problem this product is addressing

Competitor Products

Points of Difference

Materials & Suppliers

Material   ### Supplier   ### Cost

-
-
-
-
-

-
-
-
-
-

-
-
-
-
-

Pricing

$ $ $

Materials Cost   Sale Price   Margin

Overheads

Other   (Sale Price - Base Cost)

Labor

Base Cost   _____

Shipping and packaging

Note: If offering 'free shipping' remember to add this to your base cost

Marketing

Keywords

Marketing Plan Outline

Social Media Post & Graphics Ideas

Newsletter Headline & Content ideas

Promotion Ideas

Notes

Product Name

Overview

Outline of product

Specifics (weight, size)

Materials

Other (ie color, fragrance)

Standalone Product ☐   Product Range ☐

Features   Benefits

-
-
-
-
-

-
-
-
-
-

Ideal Customer / Target Market

Need / Want / Problem this product is addressing

Competitor Products

Points of Difference

Materials & Suppliers

Material	Supplier	Cost
•	•	•
•	•	•
•	•	•
•	•	•
•	•	•

Pricing

$ $ $

Materials Cost   Sale Price   Margin

Overheads

Other   (Sale Price - Base Cost)

Labor

Base Cost   _____

Shipping and packaging

Note: If offering 'free shipping' remember to add this to your base cost

Marketing

Keywords

Marketing Plan Outline

Social Media Post & Graphics Ideas

Newsletter Headline & Content ideas

Promotion Ideas

Notes

Product Name

Overview

Outline of product

Specifics (weight, size)

Materials

Other (ie color, fragrance)

Standalone Product ☐   Product Range ☐

Features   Benefits

-
-
-
-
-

Ideal Customer / Target Market

Need / Want / Problem this product is addressing

Competitor Products

Points of Difference

Materials & Suppliers

Material   Supplier   Cost

-
-
-
-
-

Pricing

$ $ $

Materials Cost   Sale Price   Margin

Overheads

Other   (Sale Price - Base Cost)

Labor

Base Cost   _____

Shipping and packaging

Note: If offering 'free shipping' remember to add this to your base cost

Marketing

Keywords

Marketing Plan Outline

Social Media Post & Graphics Ideas

Newsletter Headline & Content ideas

Promotion Ideas

Notes

Product Name

Overview

Outline of product

Specifics (weight, size)

Materials

Other (ie color, fragrance)

Standalone Product ☐   Product Range ☐

Features   ### Benefits

-
-
-
-
-

Ideal Customer / Target Market

Need / Want / Problem this product is addressing

Competitor Products

Points of Difference

Materials & Suppliers

Material	Supplier	Cost
•	•	•
•	•	•
•	•	•
•	•	•
•	•	•

Pricing

$ $ $

Materials Cost   Sale Price   Margin

Overheads

Other   (Sale Price - Base Cost)

Labor

_____

Base Cost   _____

Shipping and packaging

Note: If offering 'free shipping' remember to add this to your base cost

Marketing

Keywords

Marketing Plan Outline

Social Media Post & Graphics Ideas

Newsletter Headline & Content ideas

Promotion Ideas

Notes

Product Name

Overview

Outline of product

Specifics (weight, size)

Materials

Other (ie color, fragrance)

Standalone Product ☐   Product Range ☐

Features

-
-
-
-
-

Benefits

-
-
-
-
-

Ideal Customer / Target Market

Need / Want / Problem this product is addressing

Competitor Products

Points of Difference

Materials & Suppliers

Material	Supplier	Cost

Pricing

$ $ $

Materials Cost   Sale Price   Margin

Overheads

Other   (Sale Price - Base Cost)

Labor

Base Cost

Shipping and packaging

Note: If offering 'free shipping' remember to add this to your base cost

Marketing

Keywords

Marketing Plan Outline

Social Media Post & Graphics Ideas

Newsletter Headline & Content ideas

Promotion Ideas

Notes

Product Name

Overview

Outline of product

Specifics (weight, size)

Materials

Other (ie color, fragrance)

Standalone Product ☐   Product Range ☐

Features   Benefits

-
-
-
-
-

-
-
-
-
-

Ideal Customer / Target Market

Need / Want / Problem this product is addressing

Competitor Products

Points of Difference

Materials & Suppliers

Material	Supplier	Cost
•	•	•
•	•	•
•	•	•
•	•	•
•	•	•

Pricing

$ $ $

Materials Cost   Sale Price   Margin

Overheads

Other   (Sale Price - Base Cost)

Labor

Base Cost   _____

Shipping and packaging

Note: If offering 'free shipping' remember to add this to your base cost

Marketing

Keywords

Marketing Plan Outline

Social Media Post & Graphics Ideas

Newsletter Headline & Content ideas

Promotion Ideas

Notes

Product Name

Overview

Outline of product

Specifics (weight, size)

Materials

Other (ie color, fragrance)

Standalone Product ☐   Product Range ☐

Features

-
-
-
-
-

Benefits

-
-
-
-
-

Ideal Customer / Target Market

Need / Want / Problem this product is addressing

Competitor Products

Points of Difference

Materials & Suppliers

Material	Supplier	Cost
•	•	•
•	•	•
•	•	•
•	•	•
•	•	•

Pricing

	$		$		$
Materials Cost		Sale Price		Margin	
Overheads					
Other				(Sale Price - Base Cost)	
Labor					

Base Cost _____

Shipping and packaging
Note: If offering 'free shipping' remember to add this to your base cost

Marketing

Keywords

Marketing Plan Outline

Social Media Post & Graphics Ideas

Newsletter Headline & Content ideas

Promotion Ideas

Notes

Product Name

Overview

Outline of product

Specifics (weight, size)

Materials

Other (ie color, fragrance)

Standalone Product ☐   Product Range ☐

Features	Benefits
•	•
•	•
•	•
•	•
•	•

Ideal Customer / Target Market

Need / Want / Problem this product is addressing

Competitor Products

Points of Difference

Materials & Suppliers

Material	Supplier	Cost
•	•	•
•	•	•
•	•	•
•	•	•
•	•	•

Pricing

$ $ $

Materials Cost   Sale Price   Margin

Overheads

Other   (Sale Price - Base Cost)

Labor

Base Cost   _____

Shipping and packaging

Note: If offering 'free shipping' remember to add this to your base cost

Marketing

Keywords

Marketing Plan Outline

Social Media Post & Graphics Ideas

Newsletter Headline & Content ideas

Promotion Ideas

Notes

Product Name

Overview

Outline of product

Specifics (weight, size)

Materials

Other (ie color, fragrance)

Standalone Product ☐   Product Range ☐

Features	Benefits
•	•
•	•
•	•
•	•
•	•

Ideal Customer / Target Market

Need / Want / Problem this product is addressing

Competitor Products

Points of Difference

Materials & Suppliers

Material	Supplier	Cost
•	•	•
•	•	•
•	•	•
•	•	•
•	•	•

Pricing

$ $ $

Materials Cost   Sale Price   Margin

Overheads

Other   (Sale Price - Base Cost)

Labor

Base Cost _____

Shipping and packaging

Note: If offering 'free shipping' remember to add this to your base cost

Marketing

Keywords

Marketing Plan Outline

Social Media Post & Graphics Ideas

Newsletter Headline & Content ideas

Promotion Ideas

Notes

Product Name

Overview

Outline of product

Specifics (weight, size)

Materials

Other (ie color, fragrance)

Standalone Product ☐   Product Range ☐

Features   Benefits

-
-
-
-
-

Ideal Customer / Target Market

Need / Want / Problem this product is addressing

Competitor Products

Points of Difference

Materials & Suppliers

Material   Supplier   Cost

Material	Supplier	Cost
•	•	•
•	•	•
•	•	•
•	•	•
•	•	•

Pricing

$ $ $

Materials Cost   Sale Price   Margin

Overheads

Other   (Sale Price - Base Cost)

Labor

_____

Base Cost   _____

Shipping and packaging

Note: If offering 'free shipping' remember to add this to your base cost

Marketing

Keywords

Marketing Plan Outline

Social Media Post & Graphics Ideas

Newsletter Headline & Content ideas

Promotion Ideas

Notes

Notes